HONG KONG

BY ALON GARTY

For my parents

INTRODUCTION

Although many faces of Hong Kong have already been portrayed in countless photographs by countless photographers, the city is by no means devoid of surprise or mystery. In a city that is constantly regenerating itself, constantly in the throes of kinetic action, there are always new stories unfolding – and curious islands of stillness standing unnoticed on the margins of the tide.

Alon Garty invites you to open your eyes to the pent-up energy and obscure facets of Hong Kong life. With a penchant for exploring the nooks and crannies of the city, Alon weaves an impulsive trail through wet markets and back alleys to record the gritty dynamism of his adopted home, finding beauty in both the mundane and the sublime with his inventively angled shots. Through his lens, each scene is imbued with a life of its own, celebrating an intriguing mix of characters and the extreme contrasts that make Hong Kong such a captivating mishmash.

Hong Kong may have become a forest of gleaming skyscrapers and bamboo scaffolding, but the property tycoons have not yet completed their rout. Alon's images of the city's built environment provoke many reinterpretations of exactly what it comprises. Plainly, it is no ordinary jumble of buildings that defines Hong Kong. Behind the stereotypical blinding lights lie remarkable discoveries of quaint charm, some of which even retain a fond vestige of colonial times.

Just in case the stress of surviving in Hong Kong threatens to become too familiar, Alon uses considerable wit to make the familiar unfamiliar: tilted, top-down camera angles are drawn to accentuate the heady urban experience, whereas quiet-yet-revealing snapshots of private moments represent contemplation, escape and rest. You can sense the passion searing through these photographs of people carving out their own space, their own oasis of calm, amid the frenzy of the city. Even among seven million busy souls, it can be strangely easy to find yourself alone.

Alon Garty's rich collection of photographs takes you on a whirlwind tour of Hong Kong. Some of Hong Kong's most familiar buildings, scenarios and personalities are embraced in these images, but in a personal way that is unique to this photographer. They are a tribute to the Hong Kong he loves.

ALON GARTY was born in Tel Aviv in 1980 and was raised in Israel, Italy and France. After working in Belgium for several years, he arrived in Hong Kong in 2008. His passion for photography, however, had begun seven years earlier during his first visit to Southeast Asia. Since then, his wanderlust has taken him as far as West Africa, South America, Europe, Nepal and China.

Alon's photography is guided by the Chinese proverb 'the journey is the reward'. Always seeking new discoveries, for Alon it is the experience that counts – an attitude which infuses his unique style. Apart from documenting his travels in photographs, Alon has also written about Fiji, India and Ivory Coast for the Israeli travel magazine *Masa Olami*. His works have been exhibited in Israel, Belgium and Hong Kong, among other locations.

Hong Kong is Alon's first book.

"

I remember my first weekend in Hong Kong.

I walked into buildings covered with 'to let' signs. I went through different metal gates and took pictures of old letterboxes. The air was thick with the aroma of roast meat mixed with the smells of traditional Chinese medicine. The traffic smog pressed in as two people traded arguments in a barber shop. The heaving markets and the general stores that sell watermelons and small statues of Buddha kicked my senses into overdrive. This chaotic mishmash makes Hong Kong a big eclectic store. No matter how hard Hong Kong tries to be modern, there are always some aspects that will adamantly refuse to change.

I cherish the opportunity Hong Kong has given me to be as big as I can, to meet interesting people from every corner of the world in a welcoming and safe environment. This environment can be harsh and unforgiving sometimes, but contentment is about creating personal space and it does not necessarily have to be extravagant.

All it takes is a little creativity. "

- *Alon Garty on Hong Kong*

48

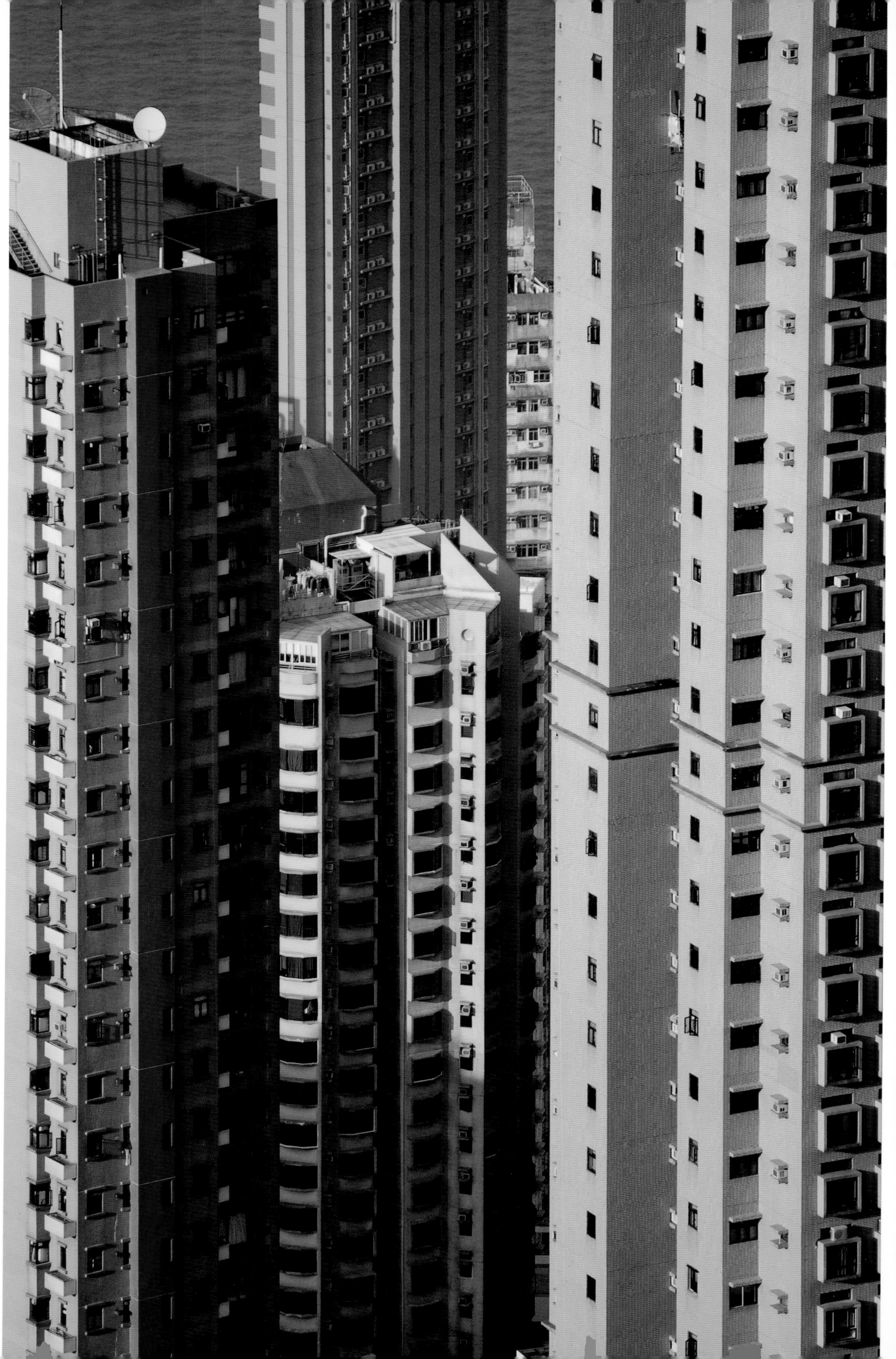

CLUB **ROMANCE**

CLUB **ROMANCE**

→ EN JOY ←
THE BEST IN TOWN
CARLSBERG
Draught Beer
FRESH TASTE
little more Stronger
H.K.$ 10,-
Each only
Cheaper than Water

→ EN JOY ←
THE BEST IN TOWN
CARLSBERG
Draught BEER
FRESH TASTE
little more Stronger
H.K.$ 10,-
Each only
Cheaper than WATER!

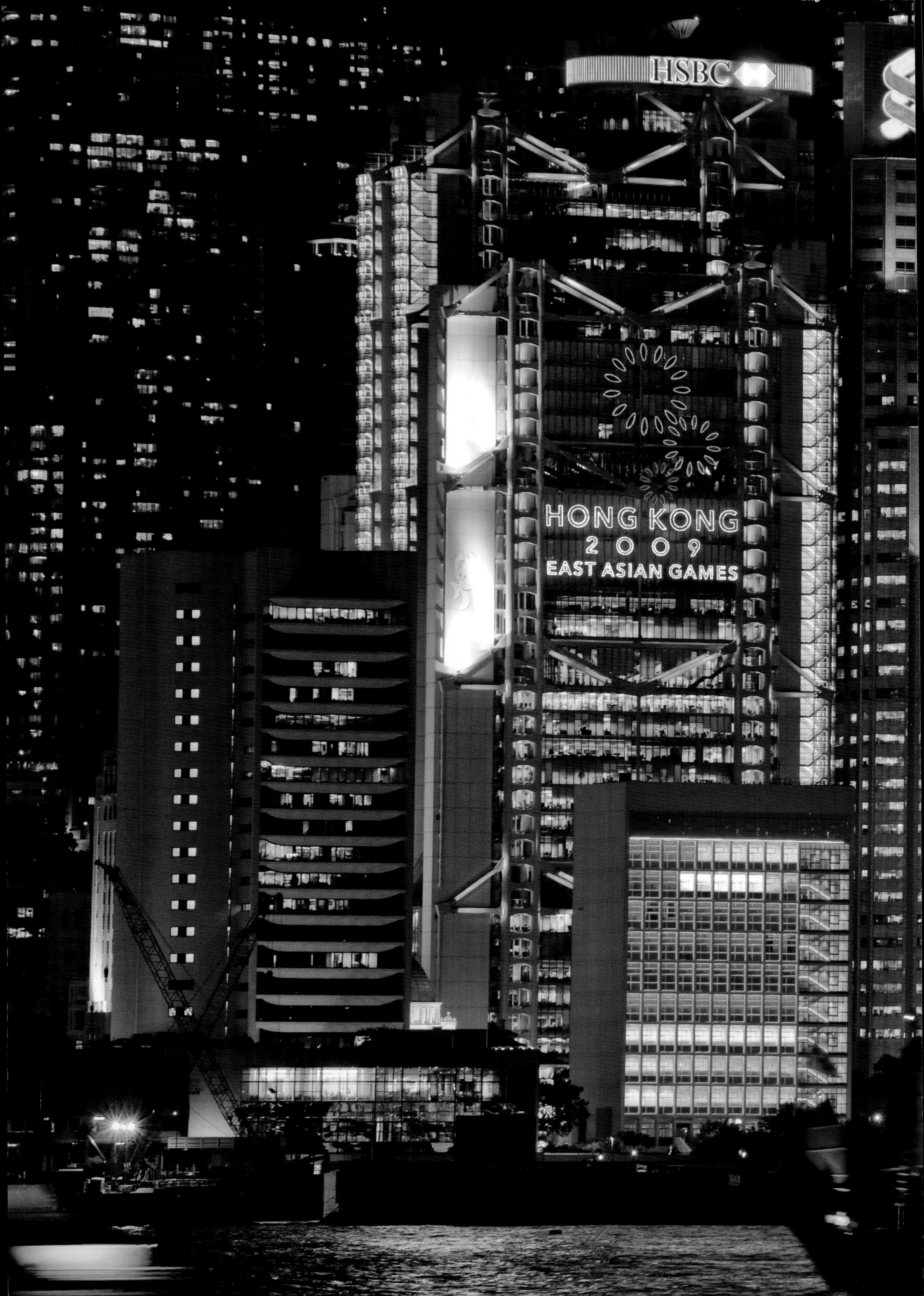
HSBC
HONG KONG
2 0 0 9
EAST ASIAN GAMES

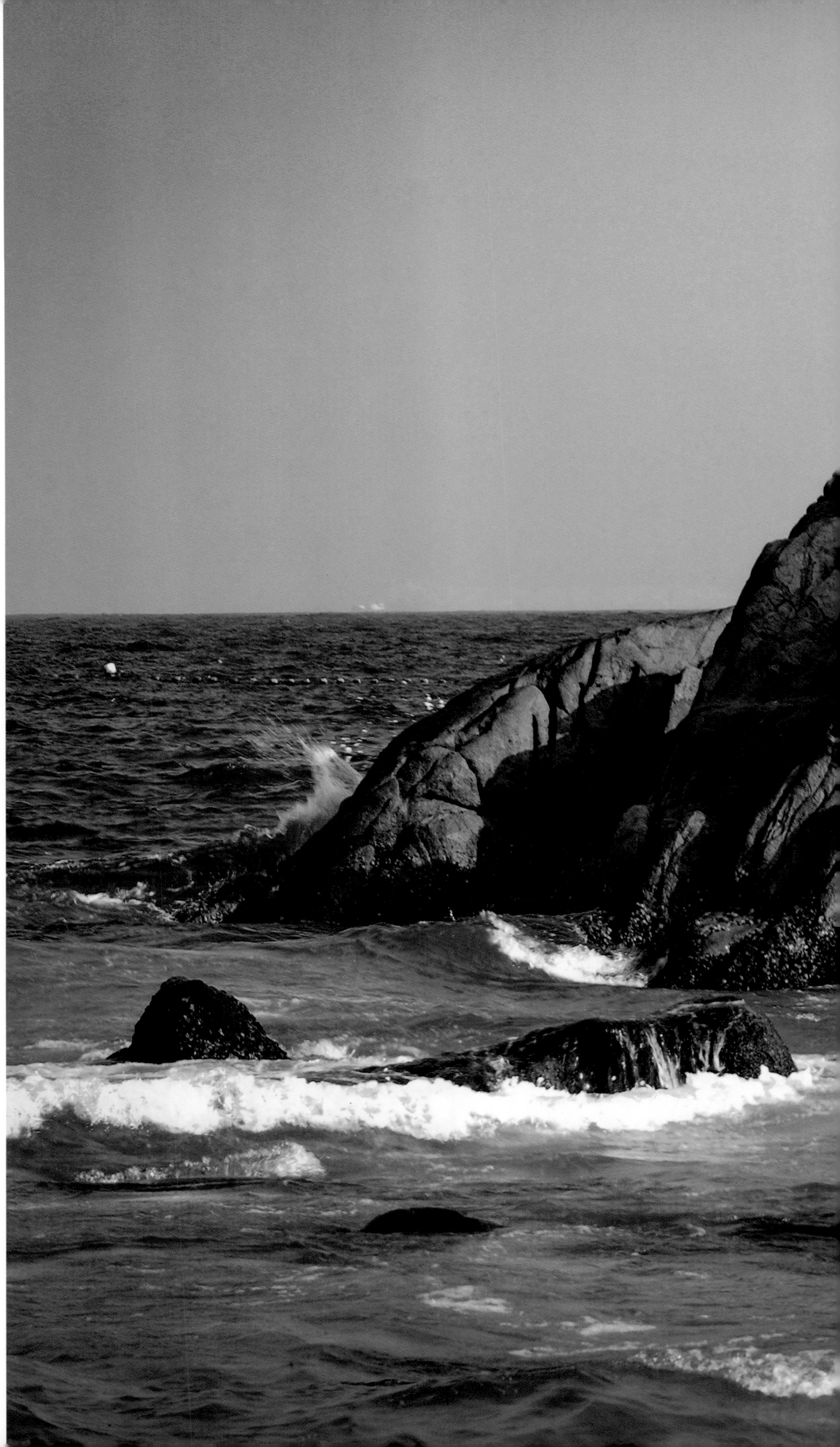

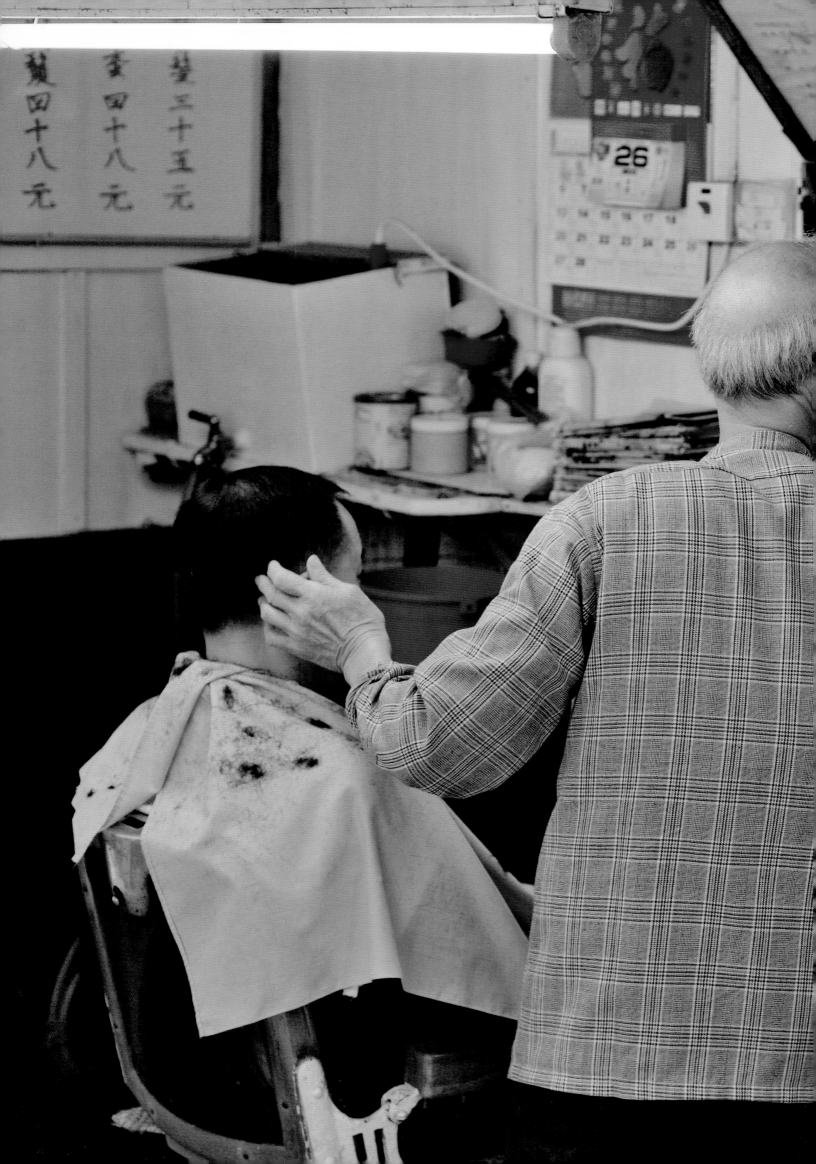

Hong Kong
by Alon Garty
www.alongarty.com

Graphic editing by AOMM Creative Limited
Graphic design by Nysreen El-Mahmoud, www.nysreen.com
Colour management by Asia One Graphic Limited
Printing by Asia One Printing Limited

Special thanks to Yohav Horesh for his valuable advice and to Haider Kikabhoy for his contribution.

asiaone

Published by Asia One Books
aopp@asiaone.com.hk
www.asiaonebooks.com

First published in May 2012

ISBN 978-988-15316-7-4